GEORGE GERSHWIN

American Musical Genius

Carin T. Ford

Enslow Publishers, Inc.
40 Industrial Road
Box 398
Berkeley Heights, NJ 07922
USA

http://www.enslow.com

Library of Congress Cataloging-in-Publication Data

Ford, Carin T.

George Gershwin : American musical genius / Carin T. Ford.

    p. cm. — (People to know today)

    Summary: ""A biography of American composer George Gershwin"—Provided
by publisher.

    Includes bibliographical references (p.) and index.

    ISBN-13: 978-0-7660-2887-6

    ISBN-10: 0-7660-2887-9

    1. Gershwin, George, 1898-1937—Juvenile literature. 2. Composers—United States—
Biography—Juvenile literature. I. Title.

    ML3930.G29F67 2009

    780.92—dc22

    [B]

                          2008003011

Printed in the United States of America

10 9 8 7 6 5 4 3 2 1

To Our Readers: We have done our best to make sure all Internet addresses in this book were
active and appropriate when we went to press. However, the author and publisher have no
control over and assume no liability for the material available on those Internet sites or on
other Web sites they may link to. Any comments or suggestions can be sent by e-mail to
comments@enslow.com or to the address on the back cover.

♻ Enslow Publishers, Inc., is committed to printing our books on recycled paper. The paper
in every book contains 10% to 30% post-consumer waste (PCW). The cover board on the
outside of each book contains 100% PCW. Our goal is to do our part to help young people
and the environment too!

Illustration Credits: AP/Wide World Press, pp. 25, 29, 47, 57; CBS/Landov, p. 77;
Courtesy of the Ira and Leonore Gershwin Trusts, pp. 6, 9, 11; © Jewish Chronicle
Ltd./HIP/The Image Works, p. 52; © Lebrecht Music & Arts/The Image Works, pp.
65, 74; © Lebrecht Music and Arts Photo Library/Alamy, pp. 42, 63, 67; Music
Division, The New York Public Library for the Performing Arts, Astor, Lenox and
Tilden Foundations, p. 41; National Portrait Gallery, Smithsonian Institute/Art
Resource, NY, p. 87; Photofest, pp. 1, 4, 34, 85, 90; Andreas Praefcke, p. 94; Time
& Life Pictures/Getty Images, p. 60.

Cover Illustration: AP/Wide World Photos

CONTENTS

George Gershwin

1
IN THE
SCHOOL YARD

Young George Gershwin did not like music. He preferred to roller-skate with his friends in the streets of New York City. Music was not something for a rough boy, George thought. Music was for girls.

But one day in 1908 when George was ten, he changed his mind about music. There was a violin recital in the auditorium of his school, P.S. 25. An eight-year-old boy named Max Rosenzweig was playing a piece of music called *Humoresque* by Antonin Dvorak.

Naturally, George was not interested. So he left school without permission to play in the school yard. This was something George did all the time. He was not a good student mainly because he was not interested in his classes.

While George was playing outside the school building,

he heard the notes coming from Max's violin. It was beautiful. George had never heard anything like it before.

He wanted to run inside to the auditorium and meet the young violinist. But if he did, the teachers would wonder why he had been outside in the first place. So George waited in the school yard for Max. He stayed there for an hour and a half. It began to rain, and George was soaked to the skin. But he continued to wait.

Finally, when the assembly was over, George went back into the school. Max, however, had left. George then found out where Max lived. Even though he was soaking wet, he walked to Max's house.

Max was not home, but Mr. and Mrs. Rosenzweig admired George's determination to meet their son. They arranged a time the two boys could get together. George said, "From the first moment we became the closest of friends."[1]

George may have enjoyed roller-skating and wrestling, but his friendship with Max was based on music. Max did not think George had the makings of a musician. With George's interest in street games, skipping

George Gershwin, c. 1908, at about ten years of age.

school, and fighting, this was not surprising. Still, from that day in the school yard, George's interest in music continued to grow.

When George was about twelve years old, a van pulled up on the street by his family's apartment on Second Avenue. The men in the van unloaded a piano and carried it to the Gershwin's second-floor home. It was meant for George's older brother, Ira, who had been taking music lessons. Ira was not especially talented at playing the piano and was not very excited about having a piano in his house.

But the experience was quite different for George. As soon as the piano was placed in the apartment, George sat down and began playing.

"I had no idea he could play," said Ira, "and found that despite his roller skating activities, the kid parties he attended, the many street games he participated in . . . he had found time to experiment on a player piano at the home of a friend on Seventh Street."[2]

George's mother saw to it that he started piano lessons right away. She did not expect much to come of it. Maybe George could play for her friends at parties, she thought.

No one could have known that George Gershwin would become not only an outstanding pianist, but also one of America's greatest and most famous composers.

2
MUSIC TAKES ROOT

George was given the name Jacob Gershwine when he was born in Brooklyn, New York, on September 26, 1898. The family's last name at the time was Gershvin, and Gershwine was probably a misspelling. George—who was never called Jacob and went by the name George from the time he was born—used the last name Gershvin until he began his musical career. Then, he changed it to Gershwin.

His parents were Morris and Rose, both Russian Jews who immigrated to the United States before they were married. Their first child was named Israel. Everyone called him Izzy and later Ira, the name he would be best known by. Ira was two years older than George. Arthur was born in 1900 and Frances, the Gershwin's only daughter, was born in 1906.

At the time George was born, there were no radios or television. Movies were featured in arcades where, for a nickel, you turned a crank in a machine and watched pictures flash in front of you. Some people had telephones, but they were not common.

As far as music, Americans enjoyed ragtime around the turn of the century. Ragtime was a popular type of truly American music, coming on the scene before jazz. Although it started out being wildly popular as dance music, it soon was just as well known as piano music. Many people bought sheet music of ragtime pieces and light operas. Often, this music was played on piano rolls on player pianos.

None of this really mattered to George, since he was not especially interested in music. He was more interested in playing rough games in the streets of his neighborhood. But he heard an automatic piano playing Anton Rubenstein's "Melody in F" when he

Morris and Rose Gershwin around the time they were married, July 21, 1895.

Piano Rolls

Piano rolls were rolls of paper with holes punched into them. Each hole related to a particular note. The placement and length of the hole changed depending on the note it represented. The roll moved over a tracker bar, which had anywhere from fifty-eight to eighty-eight holes in it—one for every key on the piano. As the hole in the paper passed over the hole of the tracker bar, it produced a sound.

was about six years old. "The peculiar jumps in the music held me rooted," George said. "To this very day, I can't hear the tune without picturing myself outside that arcade . . . standing there barefoot and in overalls, drinking it all in avidly."[1]

The Gershwins did not have a lot of money, but they were not poor either. Apartments were not expensive at the time George was growing up. Usually one could get a month's rent for free.

When George was about eight years old, he said, "I spent most of my time with the boys in the street, skating and, in general, making a nuisance of myself."[2]

This is not surprising since George was left on his own a lot as a boy. Morris was busy working sometimes as a foreman in a shoe factory or as a shoe designer. Occasionally, Morris owned restaurants and Rose worked with him, taking care of the finances. Ira, George's older brother, worked hard in school and was considered the scholar of the family. Arthur and Frances were younger than George, and a maid took care of the two of them.

Morris enjoyed running his own businesses—and he ran a lot of them. He ran a bakery, a Turkish bath, a chain of restaurants, a pool parlor, and even a gambling operation at a racetrack.[3]

Because Rose usually helped her husband in his various businesses, the family had a maid most of the time. When times were good—and Morris's businesses were going well—Rose took any extra money and invested it

Baby Arthur, the maid, a three-year-old George, Rose Gershwin, and a young Ira (left to right) enjoying a nice day out at Prospect Park, Brooklyn, c. 1901.

in diamonds. When times were not going as well, and things were rough for the Gershwin family, Rose would send Ira to a loan society to pawn the diamonds. This meant the jewelry was given as a deposit—or security—in order to borrow much needed money.

Morris may have been the head of various businesses, but Rose was the one who handled the family's finances. She made sure there was always enough money to provide everyone in the family with food and clothing—and a few extras. Rose did so well managing money, that even when times were hard she was able to send Frances to summer camp two years in a row. Rose dressed well, and the children always had money in their pockets to spend on candy or comic books.

Morris changed business ventures as quickly as George's fingers could fly on the piano keys. And Morris liked to live close to where he was working. This meant the family was constantly on the move. Ira calculated that between 1900 and 1917 the family moved twenty-eight times: they lived in twenty-five apartments in Manhattan and three in Brooklyn.

"Probably the most significant fact about our early childhood is that we were always moving," said George's brother Ira.[4]

George's parents were very different from each other. Morris—unlike Rose—was a quiet and gentle person who had very mild manners. He was easygoing and did what he could to avoid arguments. He and Rose were opposite in other ways as well. Even though Morris held a lot of jobs, he did not have a lot of ambition and he really was not too interested in making a lot of money. Rose and George seemed to be the two family members who had the inner drive to become successful, and George was certainly motivated to make a name for himself in the world of music. In short, George was the kind of person who pushed himself to be better than he already was.

George was closest to his older brother, Ira, although the boys had little in common. If George was like his mother, then Ira was more like his father. He was quiet, with a good disposition, gentle, and the kind of person who enjoyed spending time by himself, usually reading. He spent most of his weekly twenty-five-cent allowance, as well as the money he made from his mother's poker games, on books. Most Saturday nights, Rose invited relatives over to play poker, and she would send Ira to the local restaurant to get food and drink (everyone chipped in for this). Ira was allowed to keep the change.

Ira was always called Isidore by his parents. The truth is, even though his real name was Israel, he did not know this until he was thirty years old and applied for a passport. That is when he learned what name was on his birth certificate. Not only was Ira a scholar, but he also tended to be quiet and introverted, unlike George. Ira spent much of his time by himself reading. In addition to taking piano lessons, Ira enjoyed going to the theater. Ira also had a talent for drawing and painting. By the time he was fourteen, Ira was attending Townsend Hall, a school for exceptional students. His education there was preparing him for the City College of New York.

George was left to run around on his own—and this is exactly what he did. He roamed the streets, roller-skated, got into occasional fights, and stole a piece of fruit or a bagel from time to time from one of the peddlers with a pushcart who lined the streets of New York.

George had absolutely no interest in books. Street hockey and any kind of ball game filled George's days. He liked being called the roller-skating champion of his neighborhood. And whenever there was a fight in the area, George was always in the middle of it. He rarely took a beating.

He also enjoyed listening to jazz at an early age—and he came upon it by accident. One day, George was roller-skating in Harlem, a section of New York, and he heard some music coming from a club. Bandleader Jim Europe was playing jazz, and George took an instant liking to it. After that, he made a point of roller-skating to the club so he could sit on the sidewalk and enjoy the music. Many years later, Gershwin said listening to jazz at an early age influenced him to write his opera, *Porgy and Bess.*

But no one who knew George as a boy would have predicted he would grow up to be a composer and pianist. He was athletic with a wiry build. George was more interested in what games the other boys were playing than in reading books. He did not care for school, and frequently cut class. It did not help that one day in elementary school, George began drawing some pictures. When he showed his teacher what he was doing, she made fun of his picture in front of the entire class. It was Ira who was often called by one of the teachers to explain why George was not in school or had not done his homework—again.

However, after the day George heard Max Rosenzweig play his violin, everything changed. His interest in music took off and he progressed swiftly through his piano lessons. Ira was not forced to take lessons anymore—since George was doing so well—and could spend his days reading and writing.

For George, it was one piano teacher after another. Yet no matter how tight money was at times, "There was always money for piano lessons," said Rose Gershwin. "My husband always made enough money to take care of the family."[5]

The teachers simply could not keep up with George. He began with Miss Green (her first name is not known), a woman who lived in the area. Once he had gone beyond what Miss Green could teach him, George took lessons with two more teachers. Then came a Hungarian bandleader who played the piano very dramatically. The fee for each lesson was $1.50, an expensive price in those days. George started off playing music from grand operas. Within six months, he was playing "The William Tell Overture."

It was at this time that George met Jack Miller. George had begun attending concerts and Miller was the pianist of the Beethoven Society Orchestra. The two young men talked about their teachers, and Miller suggested that George meet his teacher, Charles Hambitzer.

Hambitzer was an outstanding pianist, who also played violin as well as cello. He was also a teacher with a lot of imagination. George would later call him "the first great musical influence of my life."[6]

When George met Hambitzer, he played "The William Tell Overture" for the great pianist. George played the piece with a lot of enthusiasm. When he had finished, Hambitzer jokingly said they should find George's piano teacher and shoot him. Despite his teasing, Hambitzer could tell right away that George had enormous talent. He agreed to take on George as a student, and regular lessons began right away.

George was always drawn to popular music, but Hambitzer thought it was important that George learned the classics first, such as the music of Johannes Bach and Wolfgang Amadeus Mozart. Hambitzer said, "He wants to go in for this modern stuff, jazz and what not. But I'm not going to let him for a while. I'll see that he gets a firm foundation in the standard music first."[7]

Not surprisingly, George's behavior as a music

student was quite different from his behavior as a student at the High School of Commerce. In 1912, Rose had sent George to the High School of Commerce so he could learn how to become an accountant, a person who takes care of people's money for them.

George remained disinterested in school and received poor grades. With Hambitzer, however, he was always on time and was interested in continuing his lessons far past the scheduled time. Hambitzer believed George was destined for great things in the world of music. He called his student a "genius."[8]

Hambitzer asked Edward Kilenyi to take on George as a student to give the boy more advanced knowledge of music. "The boy is not only talented, but is uncommonly serious in his love for music and in his search for knowledge," said Hambitzer. "The modesty with which he comes to his piano lessons, the respect and gratitude with which he accepts instruction—all this has impressed and touched me."[9]

George considered Hambitzer and Kilenyi as the two teachers who most influenced his development in music. He studied twice a week with Kilenyi. George was surprised to discover that Kilenyi approved of his interest in popular music. Most teachers and musicians would have felt George should focus on "serious" music or western European classical music.

But Kilenyi had a different point of view: "You will face the same difficulty all Americans do trying to have

Tin Pan Alley

Tin Pan Alley got its name because of the noise made by all the piano pounders along West Twenty-eighth Street between Fifth and Sixth Avenues. Writer Monroe Rosenfeld said the clamor sounded as if people were banging tin pans.

Because there were no regular commercial radio broadcasts, no movies with sound, and no television at that time, live musical theater was the main attraction. In Tin Pan Alley, the various music publishers hoped a performer would be interested in a single song—as demonstrated by the piano player or "pounder"—and buy it to be performed later.

their works performed," said Kilenyi, since serious American music was very rarely performed in those days. "It will bring you nearer your goal if you become a big success as a popular composer, for then conductors will come to you to ask for serious works."[10]

George now gave up street games for love of music. He filled scrapbooks full of pictures of composers such as Richard Wagner and Louis Gottschalk; he pasted in programs from recitals and concerts. Wagner was a nineteenth-century German opera composer and Gottschalk wrote lively piano works. George was learning classical music, but his interests in jazz and show tunes continued to grow. He mentioned this to Hambitzer, but the teacher still did not want George to focus on those types of music. He made sure that George's training stayed true to more classical roots.

In spite of his devotion to Hambitzer, George did not study with him that long. Historians cannot say for certain, but it seems most likely that George was a "serious" music student only until about 1916, when he was eighteen years old. Hambitzer's wife died suddenly at a young age, and the man had a breakdown. In addition to this, George decided it was time to leave high school and go to work. His interest in popular music led him to Tin Pan Alley.

3
TIN PAN ALLEY

Geoorge's life was now music. Nearly all his friends were musicians, and he was usually sitting at the piano when he was not in school.

By the time he was fifteen, George was a very accomplished pianist. Plus, George had excellent abilities of sight-reading—playing the music the very first time he saw it—and improvising. (Improvisation means playing music on the spot that is not written down.) Jazz and blues rely heavily on the musician's talent at improvising.

Although he was young, George left high school and was able to get a job in Tin Pan Alley. George wanted to get a job there very badly. But since this meant he would have to drop out of school, his mother was very much against it. She realized that he probably would not make a very good accountant, but she did not wish for him to become a musician. She did not believe he would ever be able to earn a living from music. Instead, she thought he should go into the fur business, making coats.

The two battled each other—both with their strong personalities. Morris, as usual, stayed out of the argument. He thought his children should decide for themselves what they wanted to do with their lives. George wanted nothing to do with the fur business. He would not take no for an answer. Finally, Rose had no choice but to give in. She watched her son leave school and go to work in Tin Pan Alley.

But this did not mean she was happy about it. She worried that he would not get far in the world as a musician. George's relationship with his mother was complicated. Some historians say that George adored his mother. George once said, "She is the kind of woman about whom composers write mammy songs—only *I* mean them."[1]

Yet there are many facts that show he and his mother had a rocky relationship. One problem between them was that they were so alike. Both were very proud to the point of selfishness. Though he was always a good son, George frequently found himself taking an opposing view to that of his mother.

George eventually got his way and left high school to go to work as a pianist. He had only been playing the piano four years, but George was now a professional.

Morris was very proud of George's musical

accomplishments, even if he did not know a good deal about music. He once said of George's composition, *An American in Paris*, "It is very important music—it takes twenty minutes to play."[2]

Tin Pan Alley got its name because of the loud banging sound made by all the pianos playing different songs in this one small area. At first, the name just meant this particular section of New York where musicians were playing a variety of songs throughout the day. Later, Tin Pan Alley came to mean the entire sheet music publishing industry in New York from the 1890s to the 1950s.

George's friend Ben Bloom told him he should try to get the job in the professional department for Jerome H. Remick and Company that had just opened. George was soon introduced (by Ben) to Remick's manager Moses Gumble, a man in his forties who himself had begun working as a pianist at the age of seventeen.

George had no experience, and despite his talent, he was quite young. Gumble was not sure he wanted to take a chance hiring the teenager. But once George played the piano, he got the job. He was hired as "piano pounder" for fifteen dollars a week. What the job actually consisted of was George demonstrating Remick's songs—sometimes with a singer accompanying him—in hopes that a performer on vaudeville or even a dancer would take an interest in a song and want to use it in a show.

The men in Tin Pan Alley's music industry were not only musicians; they were also businessmen. They encouraged young songwriters to imitate popular songs. At work, George sat at an upright piano in a cubicle. There, he played—one after another—songs published by Remick. These cubicles were not soundproof.

A loud racket sounded up and down the street as the pianists banged away, each one hoping the song he was playing would attract attention. Most of the songs were not particularly well written and George became bored after playing a piece a few times. He began to improvise, making the piece sound different and fancier than it was. He even tried his hand at writing his own songs when he had time.

At Remick's where George was a song plugger, he sat in a cubicle by himself. There were many cubicles, and all the pianists sat at their pianos for eight hours a day, playing the current songs put out by Remick. "Chorus ladies used to breathe down my back," said Gershwin. "Some of the customers treated me like dirt. Others were charming."[3]

Irving Caesar was a lyricist—someone who writes the words for a song—who hung around Remick's hoping to sell his lyrics. He liked George's piano playing so much, he sometimes came around just to hear him play. "His rhythms had the impact of a sledge hammer. His harmonies were years ahead of the time. I had never before heard such playing of popular music," Caesar said.[4]

Sometimes George traveled. He was occasionally

sent to other places to play Remick's songs. He visited bars, small restaurants, even the music section of department stores. He would journey to nearby cities with a vocalist. Many department stores in those days had a music section that included a piano.

George was not very happy playing for Remick's since there was very little room for the creativity that was waiting to explode within him. Yet he held the job for nearly three years. The few times he showed Gumble the songs he had written, Gumble rejected them as being too sentimental. Two of the songs George wrote then would later become known as "Nobody But You" and "Drifting Along with the Tide."

Although George was frustrated and unhappy, he was meeting a lot of people in the business, nearly all of whom were dazzled by his amazing talent on the piano. Composer Kay Swift said, "When George played . . . nobody would move, except toward the piano, and everybody held his breath."[5]

One of George's good friends was dancer Fred Astaire, who was a year younger than George, and part of a vaudeville dance team with his sister, Adele. The brother-and-sister team hoped to perform in musical theater one day. Their dreams—certainly Fred's—would come true. Fred Astaire would become the best-known name in American dance. He would go on to perform in musical films, spanning a career of seventy-six years. Many dance

The legendary dancing duo Fred and Adele Astaire pose for a photograph in 1924 during rehearsals for the Broadway musical *Lady, Be Good*.

experts consider Fred Astaire the greatest dancer of the twentieth century.

Herman Paley, a composer, also became George's friend. Before earning a living as a song-writer, Paley had been a high school teacher. Like George, he had studied piano with Charles Hambitzer. He had also studied composition, theory, and harmony.

Paley often had gatherings at his home, which included writers and musicians. Calling George a genius, Paley often invited the teenager to his home. George enjoyed being surrounded by people of similar interests and was a regular guest at these parties.

Mabel Schirmer, a friend, said: "George made the piano do things for him. When he sat down at the piano, he not only played what was written—he was improvising all the time. George made the piano laugh, he could make it sad, he could make it do anything. And when he made it laugh he chuckled and you would chuckle with him."6

George wanted to earn more money than what he was making at Remick's. So in late 1915—while the United States was involved in the fighting of World War I—he started to cut piano rolls for the player pianos.

George worked for the Standard Music Roll Company in New Jersey. The money was good: cutting six rolls on a given Saturday would bring in twenty-five dollars. He cut songs by a variety of popular composers of the day, including Irving Berlin and Jerome Kern.

Irving Berlin was born about ten years earlier than George. Berlin was a Broadway songwriter who wrote both music and lyrics for shows. Interestingly, he was never able to read music beyond the very beginner level. Still, he composed more than three thousand songs. Some of the more famous ones are "Alexander's Ragtime Band," "God Bless America," "White Christmas," and "There's No Business Like Show Business."

Jerome Kern composed songs at the same time as Berlin. He wrote the scores for more than a hundred shows and films. Some of his best known songs include "Ol' Man River," "The Way You Look Tonight," and "Long Ago and Far Away."

In 1916, George even made a roll of his own song "When You Want 'Em, You Can't Get 'Em . . . ." and an instrumental piece he wrote titled "Rialto Ripples."

George approached music publisher Harry Von

Tilzer Music Publishing Company with "When You Want 'Em, You Can't Get 'Em . . ." He hoped the song would be accepted after all the rejection he had experienced with his own work at Remick's. He was right.

George and Murray Roth, who wrote the song's lyrics, sold the song to Von Tilzer for one dollar. The money certainly was not good, but the young men were now encouraged to work on another song. They wrote "My Runaway Girl," which they thought would work well in musical theater. They performed the song for Sigmund Romberg, who composed for Broadway revues.

Romberg would later become well known for his operettas. He went on to write such popular operettas as *The Student Prince*, *The Desert Song*, and *Blossom Time*.

Many composers broke into the music business by first writing for revues. A revue was a kind of vaudeville show. Vaudeville had started to attract attention in the late 1800s. The shows it offered were wide and varied. There were dancing and singing acts, comedy, animal entertainment, and general skits.

When vaudeville first hit the scene in New Jersey in the mid-1800s, it did not do very well. But when theaters opened later in New York with vaudeville entertainment, they were successful and found a place in American musical history.

As time went on, a man named George W. Lederer became interested in making a fancier type of vaudeville show. He hired composers to write songs that were specifically for his show—not picked up from shows that had been performed elsewhere. He also had his shows in Broadway theaters, spending a lot of money on fancy—and costly—costumes and sets. It was this fancier kind of vaudeville that became the revue. The most successful of all revues were the ones put on by Florenz Ziegfeld. They were called the *Ziegfeld Follies.*

This is the business George wanted to break into. And while Romberg listened to George's song, he was more interested in listening to George play. He asked George if he would like to work with him on songs for a show called *The Passing Show of 1916.* George eagerly agreed, although Roth was not included in the invitation. George wrote "Making of a Girl" with Harold Atteridge, who worked for the show as a lyricist.

In spite of his success with Romberg, George was still experiencing mainly rejection. He teamed up with songwriter Irving Caesar to write "Good Little Tune" and "When the Armies Disband." But neither song was published.

Like George, Irving Caesar lived in New York City and was a well-known composer and lyricist. He would go on to write the words for such songs as "Swanee," "Sometimes I'm Happy," "Crazy Rhythm," and "Tea for Two."

In an instrumental piece called "Rialto Rag," George used elements of ragtime. It was published in 1917 but did not attract very much attention.

George wanted to be successful even though he was not entirely sure if he wanted to play or compose. And if he wanted to compose, what kind of music would he select?

Gershwin's colleague Irving Caesar talks to a group of children in 1987, fifty years after Gershwin's death. Caesar died on December 17, 1996, at one hundred one years old.

George enjoyed the music of songwriter Jerome Kern and, as a young man, tried to imitate him. "I followed Kern's work and studied each song he composed," said Gershwin. "I paid him the tribute of frank imitation, and many things I wrote at this period sounded as though Kern had written them himself."[7]

However, he knew he would never be successful if he continued working as a piano pounder for Remick's. In the spring of 1917, he quit, even though he had no idea what his next move would be.

"Once out of Remick's, I scarcely knew which way to turn," he said.[8]

So George pounded the streets, hoping there would be some opportunity for him to use his musical talent. Finally, after a few weeks, George landed the job of pianist at the City Theater, a vaudeville house. He was to play piano by himself during the supper show while the orchestra ate dinner. For two daytime performances, he sat on the piano bench next to the regular pianist, studying the music.

When it was time for the supper show, he played well until he came upon some music that was difficult to read—the music was not written in a way that was easy to understand. George was an excellent pianist and did the best he could. But suddenly he realized that the music he was playing was different from what the chorus was singing. In other words, George was playing one part of a song while the performers on stage were singing another. George was horrified.

There was a comedian in the show who decided to make the most of the situation. "Who told you you were a piano player?" he shouted down to George, while the audience laughed. He then continued, "You ought to be banging the drums!"[9] Now, the performers on stage joined the audience in laughing at George.

But George was not laughing. He stood up from the

piano and left the theater. The comedian continued shouting insults to the delight of the audience.

George remembered that incident as the most humiliating of his life. He never returned to that theater and had to hunt for work yet again.

George's father now ran a bathhouse. Ira, also in need of work, helped out there. But George did not want to work in a bathhouse. His dreams went much further than that. He was determined to find a job in the music business. Although he still cut piano rolls, this did not bring in enough money. So he accompanied singers in concerts from time to time. Still, he needed steady work.

When George learned that Century Theatre needed a rehearsal pianist for the revue *Miss 1917,* he hurried over to audition for the job—and he got it. In the early 1900s, there were no compact disc players or cassette players. Dancers and singers needed to perform to music, and so someone was needed to play the piano. *Miss 1917* was George's first Broadway production, and it helped give George a good understanding of what it took to put on such a show.

Miss 1917 opened in early November, but had a short run of only forty-eight performances. It was an expensive production and reviews were mixed, a combination that spelled doom for any show.

George then landed a job as piano accompanist for the Sunday Night Century Concerts. A variety of singers and dancers performed at the Century on Sundays.

When George rehearsed with singer Vivienne Segal, she chose to sing two songs George had composed and played for her—"You-oo, Just You" and "There's More to the Kiss Than the X-X-X."

Segal sang the numbers and a scout in the audience liked "You-oo" and took it to Remick's for publication. George's songs also attracted the attention of Harry Askins, who had been manager of the *Miss 1917* show. He spoke of George to Max Dreyfus, a powerful man in the music industry. He owned the T. B. Harms Company, which published such well-known composers as Victor Herbert and Jerome Kern.

Dreyfus wanted to hear the talented young composer. After George played for him and showed him a portfolio of songs he had written, Dreyfus hired him as a staff composer at thirty-five dollars a week. Gershwin was just nineteen years old.

Dreyfus said about Gershwin, "He was the kind of man I like to gamble on, and I decided to gamble."[10]

4
BIG BREAK

It was February 10, 1918, when George Gershwin joined the staff of T. B. Harms. The deal was that Gershwin would receive thirty-five dollars a week to write music. He did not have to keep regular hours, nor did he have to stick to any particular schedule. The arrangement was unusual—and it suited Gershwin perfectly. The first song he wrote for Dreyfus was "Some Wonderful Sort of Someone" in 1918.

One of the most popular stars of the stage at that time was Nora Bayes. She listened to "Some Wonderful Sort of Someone" and liked it so much she wanted it in her newest show, *Ladies First*.

Gershwin was always confident, and he asked the performer if she would also like to use "The Real American Folk Song" in her show. Bayes not only agreed to take both

A young George Gershwin in his early twenties, circa 1918–1920

songs, but she also wanted George to travel with her as the pianist.

Ira Gershwin had written the lyrics to "The Real American Folk Song," although he had signed his name Arthur Francis, after his brother and sister. Ira wanted to hear the song performed. So he took off a day from working at the Turkish baths and traveled by train to Trenton, New Jersey, where *Ladies First* was having its tryout.

But he got off at the wrong railroad station and nearly missed the show. Fortunately, he found a trolley that took him to Trenton. He arrived in time to hear Bayes sing the song. However, by the time the show reached New York, "The Real American Folk Song" had been cut.

George did not get along very well with Nora Bayes, nor was he thrilled with how the show was turning out. He wrote to his brother:

> *I have 3 songs in the show namely, "Some Wonderful Sort of Someone," "Something About Love," and "The Folk Song." "Wonderful Someone" unfortunately is misplaced, being the first song Miss Bayes does, & coming in a spot where a comedy song is expected. I will be glad if she removed it. It's not worth a nickel the way it's done now. Unless she puts it way back in the show, & has it done with the girls I'd rather have it out altogether.*[1]

Florenz Ziegfeld

Florenz Ziegfeld was enormously successful with his Follies. But he was also known for treating the people who worked for him poorly. He did not even treat the animals in his acts well. The Society for the Prevention of Cruelty to Animals closed his show, *The Dancing Ducks of Denmark*, in 1922 when it was learned that the ducks were dancing because heat was being applied to the bottoms of their feet.

Yet many famous performers worked for Ziegfeld, including George White. White began his career as a dancer in the Follies, but was best known for producing his competing musical shows, *Scandals*.

For the next ten years, Gershwin kept turning out songs. Still, Dreyfus did not take credit for Gershwin's accomplishments. He said, "A man with Gershwin's talent did not need anybody to push him ahead. His talent did all the pushing."[2]

But the two worked well together and there is little doubt Dreyfus did whatever he could to help Gershwin's career.

But that was not all he did. Gershwin toured with vaudeville performer Louise Dresser as a pianist. More of Gershwin's songs were used, as he traveled to Boston, Baltimore, and Washington, D.C., where they performed at Keith's Theatre for President Woodrow Wilson.

Once he was back in New York, Gershwin went to work for Dreyfus while also working as a rehearsal pianist, first for the Ziegfeld Follies of 1918, then Jerome Kern's *Rock-a-Bye Baby*.

While Gershwin worked on *Rock-a-Bye Baby*, he became friendly with Kern and listened to any advice he was given about the business. Gershwin continued hoping that Dreyfus would place one of his songs in a show. With that in mind—even though Dreyfus had not published anything yet of his—Gershwin worked on song after song.

He finally hit it big with his friend Irving Caesar. Modeled after the hit (at that time) called "Hindustan," the two men decided to set a song in the South. Working out the lyrics and general idea of the tune as they rode the bus to Gershwin's apartment, the men wrote the song in about fifteen minutes once they had arrived at Gershwin's place. Gershwin's father had friends over for cards and they were less than thrilled at Gershwin working out a song in the background.

Playwright S. N. Behrman said, "It was a perpetual wonder that Gershwin could do his work in the living room of this particular flat [on West One Hundredth Street], the simultaneous stamping ground of the other members of the family and the numberless relatives and visitors who would lounge through, lean on the piano, chat, tell stories, and do their setting up exercises . . ."[3]

But once they had finished the number, Gershwin's father wrapped tissue paper around a comb and "accompanied" his son in a duet. All that was needed now was a title. Finally, Caesar came up with "Swanee."

Since Gershwin was still working as a pianist for the Follies, he used the opportunity to perform it for some chorus girls and for director Ned Wayburn. Wayburn liked the song right away and told Gershwin he wanted to use it in his next show. He also wanted another of Gershwin's songs—"Come to the Moon"—for which Lou Paley had written the lyrics.

Gershwin had to wait a year to see his "Swanee" performed since the Capitol Theatre was under construction. Meanwhile, the song he had written with Caesar, "You-oo, Just You," was used in the show *Hitchy-Koo of 1918*. In other words, many Broadway shows carried songs by Gershwin during this time.

The success of Gershwin's songs and his ever-growing confidence in understanding the workings of the music business combined to make Gershwin consider writing his own show. No sooner did he put these thoughts into words than Gershwin got his chance. Dreyfus asked him to work with Edward B. Perkins, putting together an American version of the English hit revue *Half Past Eight*. Perkins wrote some of the lyrics along with Ira.

The show can be considered a learning experience for Gershwin. The reviews were not good and within a few days, some of the performers refused to appear onstage until they were paid. Perkins approached Gershwin, telling him he had to play the piano for the audience while Perkins persuaded the actors to perform.

Gershwin asked Perkins what he should play. "Some of your hits," Perkins told him. "I should have loved to have played my hits—except that I didn't have any," Gershwin said later.[4]

Although the show was a failure, Gershwin said he got a big thrill out of seeing his name on the billboard.

Gershwin's music continued to thrill other people as well as himself. He enjoyed playing the piano at the gatherings held at the home of Lou and Emily Paley. Howard Dietz, a lyricist, lived on the floor below the Paleys and got annoyed that on Saturday nights, the chandelier would shake because of the thumping of the piano above him and his wife.

Dietz finally decided to complain to the Paleys one Saturday night. He marched upstairs and banged on the Paleys' door. Someone opened it, and Dietz walked inside.

"About forty people were sitting on the floor around the grand piano at which a dark-haired chap was playing and singing," said Dietz. "He was vastly entertaining. I took a seat on the floor." When Dietz's wife got tired of waiting for him, she appeared at the Paleys' door only to have her husband gesture for her to come inside. "We never got to the theater [that night]," Dietz said, "and we stopped bothering about our chandelier. We became regulars at the Saturday nights at the Lou Paleys to hear George Gershwin."5

Gershwin plugged away at writing songs and from time to time they were used in shows. Meeting Irving Berlin, Gershwin asked to be hired as the famous songwriter's secretary, writing down the music for Berlin.

But after Gershwin demonstrated his talent on the

piano with some of his own songs, Berlin said, "Stick to writing your own songs, kid."[6] He believed Gershwin was too good to work for somebody else.

Gershwin got his big break when he was twenty. He was hired by Alexander A. Aarons to compose the songs for a new show called *La, La Lucille*. Some of Gershwin's songs that were used in the show are "Nobody but You," "Tee-Oodle-Um-Bum-Bo," and "From Now On." This was a big break for George; it was his first full Broadway score.

The show was successful, running from late May to late August 1919 and eventually closing because of an actors' strike. While the reviews were good, most of the attention was focused on the show—not Gershwin's songs.

Only a couple months after *La, La Lucille* closed, "Swanee" was finally ready to be heard. Renovations to the Capitol Theatre were complete and "Swanee" was used in a stage number that included a large band and fifty dancers who had electric lights in their shoes.

The audience seemed to enjoy the song, but for the most part, no one was interested in buying the sheet music to "Swanee." Gershwin and Caesar even bought the music themselves in hopes of encouraging other people to do the same. Their plan, however, did not work.

It seemed as though "Swanee" was destined to disappear from the music industry, until Gershwin attended a party one night for the popular performer Al

Jolson. Gershwin found himself sitting at the piano—which was where he usually wound up at parties—and began playing a number of his songs, including "Swanee." Jolson heard the song and liked it right away. He told Gershwin he wanted to perform the song in his show *Sinbad*, which was touring. He also recorded it in January 1920.

Jolson's recording turncd "Swanee" into a hit. His recording—and the sheet music for the song—sold millions of copies. It brought in ten thousand dollars in royalties that year.

For Gershwin, the success of "Swanee" made his name known throughout the music industry. He earned enough money from that one song that now he could focus on writing musical scores for shows, rather than individual songs.

Gershwin approached George White who had put on a revue called *George White's Scandals of 1919* the year before. Gershwin suggested that

The cover of the "Swanee" vocal score features Al Jolson, the man who brought Gershwin his first major success.

he write the music for the *Scandals of 1920*. White, impressed with "Swanee," quickly agreed.

Gershwin happily accepted White's offer to compose for *Scandals*. It was a great opportunity—even if the money was not especially good. Gershwin received fifty dollars a week. That eventually went up to seventy-five dollars and later one hundred twenty-five dollars.

Still, *Scandals* attracted a large and a diverse audience. And that meant a lot of people were hearing Gershwin's music.

George White's *Scandals* had thirteen different shows between 1913 and 1939. The *Scandals* were a form of the revue, with a number of sketches and musical acts.

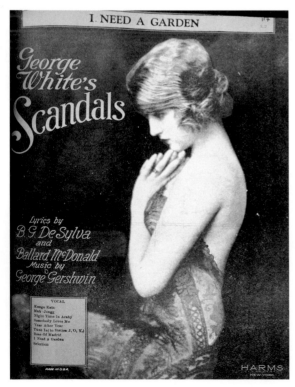

This was the most popular form of musical theater in the early 1900s.

Gershwin worked as composer for five of White's *Scandals*. In the 1922 *Scandals*, Gershwin had his first try at opera. It was only one act and titled *Blue Monday Blues*, although a few years later it was renamed

The vocal score for "I Need a Garden" from George White's *Scandals*, c. 1923–1924.

135th Street. Gershwin wrote the score in one week. As was common at that time, it was performed by white actors who had painted their faces black.

Gershwin was only twenty-four, and for someone so young, it was a bold step to take. Few composers of any age would try to write an opera for musical theater—much less in only a few days.

The critics did not like *Blue Monday Blues*, and the opera was only performed once—on opening night. But it helped lay the foundation for Gershwin's operatic masterpiece, *Porgy and Bess*, that would come thirteen years down the road.

While some thought it strange that Gershwin was attempting to mix opera with a musical revue, it did not seem odd to Gershwin. He was always experimenting, always pushing himself as a composer. He never performed a piece at the piano the same way twice. It was all music to Gershwin and the category or type merely determined the form it took. He did not divide music into "serious" or "popular."

Gershwin would go on to write for White's shows for five years in all. Two of the better known songs to come out of the collaboration are "I'll Build a Stairway to Paradise" and "Somebody Loves Me."

Lyricist Buddy DeSylva worked with Gershwin for many years and their partnership included many hit numbers. The song, "I'll Build a Stairway to Paradise" was created after DeSylva mentioned a line he liked from another one of Gershwin's unpublished songs. The song ended, "'I'll build a staircase to Paradise, [w]ith a new step ev'ry day.'"[7] DeSylva worked with George and Ira Gershwin one evening, trying to come up with a song for George White. The three men based an entirely new song around that one line, changing "staircase" to "stairway."

White loved the song and built an entire production around it in his revue. There was a very wide, shiny white stairway with dancers—dressed in black—performing up and down the steps. Meanwhile, Paul Whiteman's orchestra was set up on the stage, creating a lovely and exciting number for the audience.

When Gershwin wrote "Somebody Loves Me" for one of the *Scandals*, Morris Gershwin told him a while later how much he liked one of the songs from that show. Gershwin sat down at the piano and played "Somebody Loves Me," which was the big hit from *Scandals*. He assumed that was the song his father meant.

Morris told Gershwin that was not the song he meant. Gershwin then continued playing, until he had played every song from the show. "It must be something from another show," Gershwin told his father, "because I played everything there is." He remained sitting at the piano while his father scratched his head in puzzlement. Without thinking, Gershwin's fingers quietly repeated the song "Somebody Loves Me." Morris cried out, "That's it, that's it. Why didn't you play it for me in the first place?"[8]

George and his brother Ira had their first published song called "Real American Folksong" during this time. And although Gershwin still continued working on other productions, he had a fairly secure spot on Broadway.

5

A SERIOUS MUSICIAN

In the early 1920s, the Harlem Renaissance was taking place. The Harlem Renaissance was a time when African-American art, literature, music, and culture burst onto the scene and thrived. It was led by black Americans living in Harlem, New York.

Some composers, such as Gershwin, were not about to be left out of what the Harlem Renaissance had to offer. "Harlem is a sort of breeding place for musical ideas, but most of them are left in a kind of germinal state," said Gershwin. "You can find new rhythm, even richer harmonies there, but the germs are left for outsiders to pick up and develop."[1]

While this was occurring, Gershwin was working with DeSylva on the score for George White's *Scandals*. DeSylva knew Gershwin hoped to do more with his career than write songs for revues. He suggested Gershwin write a short opera set in Harlem.

Gershwin liked the idea, and it did not seem impossible to him. After all, *Shuffle Along*, which was an all-black show, had been hugely successful the year before. Writing a jazzy opera appealed to Gershwin. Not only would it be different musically from everything he had been doing, but it would also allow Gershwin to stretch his talents.

The idea was to put the mini-opera into White's *Scandals*. Gershwin and DeSylva went to work.

"So DeSylva sat down with his pencil and I dug down and found a couple of suitable tunes and we began writing," Gershwin said.[2]

They worked on it for five days. When the show opened, the audience and the critics did not like the opera, *Blue Monday Blues*. White took it out of the show after its opening

Gershwin's collaborator Buddy DeSylva sits at the piano with his wife at his side in 1941.

night in New York, because he thought it made the audience too depressed.

The following year, Gershwin was invited to travel to London and compose the music for a show called *Rainbow.* Gershwin's name was known in England because of the popularity of his song "Swanee." The show opened in April 1923, and from there, Gershwin traveled to Paris with DeSylva and Jules Glaenzer. After a few weeks, he returned to the United States.

Gershwin studied with Rubin Goldmark in 1923. Goldmark was a well-known pianist and also a composer, not to mention the teacher of Aaron Copland, a famous American composer. Goldmark was head of the composition department of the Juilliard School of Music. He only taught Gershwin a handful of lessons.

Gershwin had a casual approach to studying music, and Goldmark was a more exacting personality. Once, he instructed Gershwin to do some exercises in harmony. Gershwin waited until the last minute before doing these exercises. In fact, he used part of the movement of a string quartet he had written years earlier.

Yet he told Goldmark he had just written the piece. Goldmark commented, "It's plainly to be seen that you have already learned a great deal of harmony from me!"[3]

He performed that year in Aeolian Hall with singer Eva Gauthier. In the recital, Gershwin played several American songs, including his own "I'll Build a Stairway to Paradise" and "Swanee." This was Gershwin's debut at a highly regarded concert hall in New York. The songs would one day be considered jazz, and Gershwin would go on to explore that category of music even further.

Paul Whiteman wanted to put on a concert called An Experiment in Modern Music. Whiteman was an orchestra leader, although he started out as a violin and viola player. After a time, he became the leader of a jazz band. When the band moved to New York City, Whiteman had the group make recordings that grew in popularity over the years. He became well known throughout the country and was one of the most popular bandleaders of the decade. The concert was to demonstrate jazz in a concert form, which many critics at that time dismissed. But Whiteman's band specialized in such "symphonic" arrangements of jazz.

An Experiment in Modern Music was to be held at the Aeolian Hall, and Whiteman wanted Gershwin to write a piece for the program.

Yet Gershwin was surprised to read in a newspaper five weeks before the concert that "George Gershwin is at work on a jazz concerto . . ."[4]

After all, Gershwin and Whiteman had only talked about such a piece in general terms. Gershwin called Whiteman the next day, telling him he would not be able to write a jazz concerto or any other kind of piece. He was busy with his show *Sweet Little Devil* (also known as *A Perfect Lady*), a musical he was writing with lyricist DeSylva, which would soon be opening on Broadway.

Whiteman would not give up. Finally, Gershwin said perhaps he could write a free-form sort of piece—like a rhapsody. He began writing on January 7, whenever he was not busy with the show.

At first, Gershwin wanted to call the piece *American Rhapsody*. But Ira had just visited an art gallery, where he had seen the works of the American artist James Whistler. Whistler's paintings had such titles as *Nocturne in Black and Gold* and *Arrangement in Gray and Black*. Taking Ira's advice, the composition was renamed *Rhapsody in Blue*.

No one is sure exactly how long it took Gershwin to write the rhapsody, but it was somewhere between one and one-half to three weeks.

"There had been so much chatter about the limitations of jazz," said Gershwin. "I resolved, if possible, to kill that misconception with one sturdy blow . . . No set plan was in my mind—no structure to which my music would conform. The rhapsody, as you see, began as a purpose, not a plan."[5]

Gershwin said he put together the outline of *Rhapsody in Blue* while on the train headed for Boston on January 7, 1924.

"It was on the train, with its steely rhythms, its rattly-bang that is so often stimulating to a composer (I frequently hear music in the very heart of noise) that I suddenly heard—even saw on paper—the complete construction of the Rhapsody from beginning to end," Gershwin said.[6]

He was going to Boston for the tryout of *Sweet Little Devil*, which was due to open in the Astor Theater in New York on January 21.

Gershwin wrote *Rhapsody in Blue* in his parents' house where his younger siblings lived as well. He would work with Ira near him at an upright piano in a back room of the apartment. "All at once I heard myself playing a theme that must have been haunting me inside, seeking outlet," he said. "No sooner had it oozed out of my fingers than I knew I had it."[7]

Once completed, the *Rhapsody in Blue* was worked on further at rehearsals that were held at Palais Royal nightclub. Whiteman's band played a revue there and then worked on Gershwin's piece. Occasionally some music critics came to listen in on rehearsals. If they knew Gershwin at all, they only knew him as a young composer who had written some show tunes. Most of them liked *Rhapsody* as soon as they heard it. If they did not, they at least admired how energetic it was.

Rhapsody in Blue is a piece of music that combines both classical and jazz elements. Although Gershwin wrote the original composition for piano, he had Ferde Grofe orchestrate it. Most people are more familiar with the full orchestra version, and it has become one of the most famous of all American concert works.

The concert was finally held on February 12, 1924, at Aeolian Hall because Carnegie Hall—which could hold more than twice as many people—was already

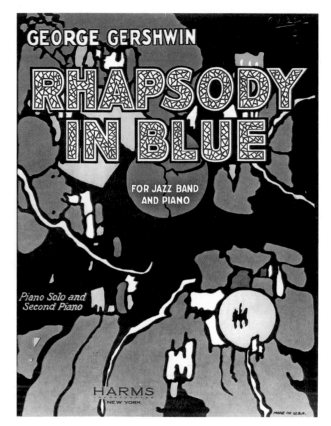

The original cover for the sheet music to 1924's *Rhapsody in Blue*. It is one of Gershwin's most famous works.

booked. Since the concert was aiming to look at the development of American music, it began with an older jazz composition called *Livery Stable Blues*.

Throughout the first half of the concert, the audience had alternated between enthusiasm and mild boredom. By the end of the second half, it seemed as if the audience was losing interest.

That is when Gershwin came out. His dark hair was combed back off his forehead. He was wearing a gray suit with a stiff white shirt. He sat down at the piano and the piece began with the now-famous swoop of the clarinet. Gershwin had not actually written down all the music for his own part—he improvised much of it.

When the rhapsody ended, the audience exploded in applause. According to one critic, they were "wild, even frantic."[8]

Some critics though found fault with the piece,

claiming it had an uncertain structure. But nearly every one of them agreed that, overall, the melody and rhythm were new and exciting, and Gershwin was a composer from whom they would hear more.

After the *Rhapsody* had its premiere, composer Arthur Schwartz said, "It was a great day . . . But while George was still taking bows to applause that should have been far more shattering, I remember saying to myself: "From now on, this revolutionary composition will influence the whole future of serious music in America."[9]

And more than one critic also noted that Gershwin's piano playing was brilliant. From Gershwin's point of view, the Experiment in Modern Music had been an outstanding success.

6

A BUSY
YOUNG MAN

Without realizing it, Gershwin and his *Rhapsody in Blue* helped bring popular music to the concert hall where only "serious" music had been played before. Through his talent, Gershwin helped the American composer win respect— and he helped his music get an audience. Gershwin was unique among American composers in this respect. His broad musical scope and popularity made him successful in many different categories, such as songwriting, Broadway musicals, opera, and concert music.

"Many persons thought the *Rhapsody* was only a happy accident," said Gershwin. "Well, I went out, for one thing, to show them that there was plenty more where that had come from. I made up my mind to do a piece of absolute music."[1]

When Gershwin was asked what he was trying to do in the rhapsody, he said, "I tried to express our manner of living, the tempo of our modern life."[2]

With its wildly successful debut, *Rhapsody in Blue* was brought to audiences throughout the country. Whiteman's concert was presented a few times in New York—including a performance at Carnegie Hall—as well as Pittsburgh, Cleveland, Indianapolis, and St. Louis.

Gershwin left the tour after performing in St. Louis in May 1924, although he did make a recording of *Rhapsody in Blue* the following month. One of the reasons he left Whiteman was to work on the *Scandals of 1924* for George White. The revue was set to open at the end of June and included the popular song "Somebody Loves Me." Gershwin also was to head to London a few weeks later to work on a new show there.

"George's drive had nothing to do with money or the lack of it," said Ira Gershwin. "He never knew how much money he had in the bank. He was really doing what he did because he felt he had to do it, whether or not it would bring him success."[3]

Gershwin spent the summer in London working on *Primrose*, which wound up having a very successful run of more than 250 performances. While he was in England, arrangements were made for Gershwin to write a musical that would star his friends, the famous dance team of Fred Astaire and his sister Adele. When

Gershwin crossed the Atlantic to return to the United States in the fall, he began serious work on the show *Lady, Be Good!*

One of the best known songs from this show is "Fascinating Rhythm," for which Gershwin had composed a few bars while he was in London. When Gershwin first played the number for his brother, Ira said, "For God's sake, George, what kind of lyrics do you write to a rhythm like that?" Some music historians say the song's title—and opening lyrics—came about simply because as Ira listened to the music, he commented, "It's a fascinating rhythm."[4]

Gershwin liked the title as well as the dance routine the Astaires choreographed. They were unable to find a decent ending, however. Gershwin watched them one day during a rehearsal, and suggested a complicated combination of steps. The Astaires tried and thought it was just right; they followed Gershwin's advice.

Lady, Be Good! was successful even though it was the fortieth musical put on in New York that year. One critic for the *New York Herald-Tribune* wrote: "When . . . they sang and danced 'Fascinating Rhythm' the callous Broadwayites cheered them as if their favorite halfback had planted the ball behind the goal posts after an eighty-yard run. Seldom has it been our pleasure to witness so heartfelt, spontaneous, and so deserved a tribute."[5]

Gershwin was no different from other composers of musicals at that time in that he did not really care much

George Gershwin (left) sits next to his brother Ira in this undated photograph. First collaborating in 1924, the songwriting duo soon left their mark in American musical theatre.

about the show's story.[6] He basically looked for places in the show where songs would work best, and many times took into account who was starring in the show.

Gershwin was a busy young man of twenty-five. "He had such a fluency at the piano and so steady a surge of ideas that any time he sat down just to amuse himself something came of it," said Oscar Levant, a pianist and composer. "Actually, this is how he got most of his ideas—just by playing. He enjoyed writing so much because, in a sense, it was play for him—the thing he liked to do more than anything else."[7]

Gershwin loved what he did but he never tried to hide the fact that he considered it hard work. "I can think of no more nerve-wracking . . . task than making music," he said. "The composer does not sit around and wait for an inspiration to walk up and introduce itself. What he substitutes for it is nothing more than talent plus his knowledge."[8]

Gershwin did have certain hours—even certain seasons—in which he preferred composing. Since he was usually out at night, he never composed in the morning.

He liked writing at night, and it did not bother him if there were many people nearby making a lot of noise. "Often I have written my tunes with people in the same room playing cards in the next," he said. "When I find myself in the desired mood, I can hold it until I finish the song."[9]

As for his best seasons for composing, Gershwin

preferred fall and winter. He enjoyed being outdoors and preferred playing golf and tennis in the warmer months.

In the middle of 1925, Gershwin was the first composer to make the cover of *Time* magazine. The publication was then two years old.

After composing the songs for the not-very-successful show *Tell Me More*, Gershwin sailed back to London where the same show would be opening on the other side of the Atlantic Ocean. It did far better in England, which freed Gershwin up to travel to Paris. At this time, Gershwin was already at work on his next musical, *Tip-Toes*, and he was putting together ideas for a *New York Concerto*. Gershwin was to be the piano soloist for seven performances of the concerto, which would be performed by the New York Symphony. The orchestra was three times the size of the Whiteman band. Confident as Gershwin was, he knew writing the concerto would be no small task.

Successful as he was, Gershwin was still living at home—and more importantly, composing at home. But now, between the difficult concerto and the musical, Gershwin decided to rent two rooms in a hotel. This way, he would be able to work without being disturbed by his mother's friends, his father's card games, and his younger siblings' comings and goings. But with so many admirers—and even visiting relatives—Gershwin was not left in peace and quiet.

George Gershwin made the cover of the July 20, 1925 issue of *Time*.

When he was invited to spend time at the peaceful Chautauqua Institute in upstate New York, Gershwin accepted. Chautauqua is a community for artists in northern New York. Visitors travel there to learn and work on art, music, and literature.

In spite of having his own cottage and working hours away from Manhattan, Gershwin still had to deal with piano students stopping by. He needed to get his work done, yet Gershwin was good-natured and always agreed to play and sing for visitors.

"I've worked with quite a lot of composers," said composer Yip Harburg. "And [George's] method of composing was the nearest to playfulness that I've ever known. Most composers sit down at the piano and say a little prayer: please God, let me have it. But George never did. George sat down at the piano as if he were going to have fun with it."[10]

Eventually, the concerto was completed and *Concerto in F* made its debut in December 1925. Carnegie Hall was packed—Gershwin's name by this time was enough to draw large crowds.

And the crowds loved it. Gershwin was congratulated by friends, family, and other composers—who also complimented his piano skill. Many at this time thought Gershwin should now focus on serious music—another concerto, symphonies, and operas.

After Gershwin played his *Six New Piano Preludes*, his friend Kay Swift said, "The preludes are swell pieces and he played them beautifully, with a lot of spirit and determination."[11]

But Gershwin seemed most interested in doing it all. He continued working on shows, as well as pushing himself to study all aspects of musical composition. Meanwhile, the musical *Tip-Toes* was a solid hit, producing such songs as "Sweet and Low-Down" and "That Certain Feeling."

Here are a few days out of Gershwin's life in December 1925 to show how hectic his schedule was:

December 3: He performed his *Concerto in F* at Carnegie Hall

December 28: His musical *Tip-Toes* opened on Broadway

December 29: His composition *Blue Monday Blues* was given the new title *135th Street* and performed at Carnegie Hall as part of Paul Whiteman's Second Experiment in Modern Music.

December 30: Gershwin, with lyrics by Oscar Hammerstein, had *Song of the Flame* open on Broadway.

Gershwin enjoyed juggling many projects at once and had no problem composing in the middle of noise and commotion. But every now and then, he would go back to renting rooms in the Whitehall Hotel to be able to focus more easily on all his work.

While Gershwin composed just one musical in 1926, it would be three years before he put together his next big orchestra piece.

With all this fame and attention at a young age, it is easy to understand why many people thought Gershwin was conceited. But his relatives and friends who knew him well did not think it was conceit. They believed Gershwin saw himself realistically, just as he was—good points and bad points.

"To me, George was a little sad all the time because he had this compulsion to work," said Ira Gershwin. "He never relaxed. He had to be doing something all the time . . . with George, everything had to have some end of keeping him busy."[12]

LOOKING FOR A BOY

ALEX A. AARONS and VINTON FREEDLEY
present
THE NEW MUSICAL COMEDY

"Tip-Toes"

MUSIC BY GEORGE GERSHWIN
BOOK BY GUY BOLTON
AND FRED THOMPSON
LYRICS BY IRA GERSHWIN

Dances and Ensembles by
SAMMY LEE
Play directed by
JOHN HARWOOD

Looking For A Boy
Nightie Night
That Certain Feeling
Sweet And Low-down
These Charming People
When Do We Dance
Nice Baby

HARMS
NEW YORK

The score cover for 1925's musical comedy *Tip-Toes*.

7

GERSHWIN
IN PARIS

ady, Be Good!, the musical starring Fred and Adele Astaire, was a hit in England as well as in the United States. Gershwin next began working on the show that would eventually be known as *Oh, Kay!* He and Ira had been working steadily on the score when one day, Ira was rushed to the hospital with appendicitis. He had to remain there for six weeks (there were no antibiotics in those days) and was constantly begging the doctors and nurses to allow him to leave: "They're waiting for me to finish the lyrics!"[1]

Finally, he was able to return to work, although with not quite so much energy as before.

Gershwin had come up with one song in the show as a number in a quick rhythm. But then he played it one day at a much slower tempo—and preferred it that way. The song was titled "Someone to Watch Over Me" and is one of Gershwin's most famous.

Oh, Kay! opened November 8, 1926, and ran for 256 performances over eight months. In addition to "Someone to Watch Over Me," the show includes the songs "Do, Do, Do" and "Clap Yo' Hands." While *Oh, Kay!* ran in New York, *Lady, Be Good!* and *Tip-Toes* were playing to large crowds in London.

Never the kind of person to sit still, Gershwin decided to write another serious piece of solo piano music. This piece was actually three numbers or preludes. Once this was written, Gershwin went to work on a political operetta called *Strike Up the Band.* The title song came to

Gertrude Lawrence performs the song "Oh, Kay!" from the 1926 musical of the same name.

Fred Astaire

Fred Astaire was born Frederick Austerlitz, in 1899 in Nebraska. When he was only six, he was performing onstage with his sister Adele. Brother and sister performed on Broadway and on the London stage through the 1920s. But Astaire is most famous for the movies he made—many of them with scores by Gershwin—with dancer Ginger Rogers. Astaire made thirty-one musical films in his seventy-six-year career and is considered by many dance critics to be the greatest dancer who ever lived.

Gershwin in a dream. This had happened to him before—but rarely could he remember the dream when he woke up. This was one time his memory served him well.

Strike Up the Band was not a success, mainly because the story was very different from the typical musical comedy of the day. The songs were not written with the idea that they might become hits, and there were no well-known actors in the show. The story was a political satire— why man feels it necessary to go to war.

But as usual, Gershwin was too busy to let a failure hold his attention for long. He was working on the show *Funny Face*, which included the songs "'S Wonderful," "Clap Yo' Hands," and "How Long Has This Been Going On?"

Written once again for the Astaires, the show had the magical combination of Gershwin's music and the Astaires' dancing. But *Funny Face* had not been doing well leading up to its New York opening. However, Gershwin kept working away at it—adding new songs,

The score cover of 1927's *Funny Face* starring Fred and Adele Astaire.

revising others. He was determined, as always, to give 100 percent to the show.

It finally opened in New York on November 22, 1927. The critics raved about it. Fred Astaire said, "The overall something was there. What a pleasant surprise! Having gone through a series of mishaps and revisions on the road, we simply didn't know what we had."[2]

Reviewer Alexander Woollcott wrote, "I do not know whether George Gershwin was born into this world to write rhythms for Fred Astaire's feet or whether Fred Astaire was born into this world to show how the Gershwin music should really be danced. But surely they were written in the same key, those two."[3]

On the heels of *Funny Face* came another musical, *Rosalie*. Now Gershwin had two shows running on Broadway at the same time and he was ready for a break. Gershwin decided to change location and head for Europe. He took his last trip to Europe in March 1928.

He traveled to London and attended a show his brother had written the lyrics for. He also saw a British performance of *Oh, Kay!*

His sister, Frances, went with George (and Ira and Ira's wife, Lenore Stravinsky) to a party in Paris, where they met Cole Porter, composer of the song "Night and Day." When Porter heard Frances sing, he offered her a spot in his revue. Frances remained in Paris while Geroge went to Berlin, Germany, and Vienna, Austria. He returned to see his sister in the show. She began her act with some lines Porter had written just for her: "I happen to be the sister of a rhythm twister, No doubt you know him as Mister George Gershwin."[4]

George accompanied Frankie on the piano on opening night. Together they performed "The Man I Love," "Embraceable You," "Do, Do, Do," and "Oh, Gee! Oh, Joy!" Several producers who came to hear the show offered Frankie roles in their own musicals, but George—acting like Frankie's father—would not allow it.

He also decided to work on a different type of music. What he had in mind was *An American in Paris*. It would become one of his best-known compositions.

Traveling through Paris with Frances, Ira, and Ira's wife, George was busy sightseeing and socializing, but he still found time to work on *An American in Paris* in the hotels where he stayed.

In Paris, Gershwin was also interested in studying

with the famous music teacher, Nadia Boulanger, who was the teacher of composer Aaron Copland. To Gershwin's surprise, Boulanger turned him down. She did not want him as a student. She listened to him play and thought he had such a natural gift for music that academic lessons from her might ruin his talent.

An American in Paris was a ballet, and, in typical Gershwin fashion, it would not be the kind of ballet with tutus and crinolines. Gershwin was writing a "real" dance piece that included street scenes. He decided to look for taxi horns used by French cabdrivers. He visited several auto body shops until he found the ones with just the right pitch for some of his scenes.

An American in Paris was "really a rhapsodic ballet, [that] is written very freely and is the most modern music I've yet attempted," Gershwin wrote. "The opening part will be developed in typical French style . . . though the tunes are all original."[5]

Gershwin returned to the United States still working on his ballet and also putting together a new musical, *Treasure Girl.* Although the show was not very successful, Gershwin was busy getting *An American in Paris* ready for its premiere.

Gershwin said his idea for the ballet was "to portray the impressions of an American visitor in Paris as he strolls about the city, listens to various street noises, and absorbs the French atmosphere."[6]

Each section of the piece represents an experience

an American might have in Paris. For example, the composition opens with an American walking down the famous street, the Champs-Elysees. The American suddenly feels homesick for his home country, and a blues theme kicks in. When he comes upon another American, a Charleston theme is played. The Charleston was a very popular kind of ballroom dance in the United States in the 1920s. When the American finally decides to enjoy all that Paris has to offer, there is a walking theme.

An American in Paris opened at Carnegie Hall on December 13, 1928. Gershwin's whole family along with many friends attended the performance. The audience applauded wildly and many critics thought the piece was a gem of modern music. According to critic Leonard Leibling, the composition was "merrily, rollicking appealing music . . . Anyone who dislikes this piece is not an American."[7]

Even the reviews that were poor—calling it dull or silly—were kept by Gershwin. In the *New York Telegram*, Herbert Peyser called *An American in Paris*, "nauseous clap trap, so dull patchy, thin, vulgar long winded and inane . . . Even as honest jazz the whole cheap and silly affair seemed pitifully futile and inept."[8]

Gershwin did not mind when critics did not give him good reviews. He was always working on developing his music. Each piece he wrote helped move him on to the next. In other words, he seemed to build on what he had done before. Gershwin knew when his compositions had weak spots; he also knew he had worked hard and done his best. He spent no time looking back. Gershwin was always looking forward.

Gershwin had always toyed with the idea of writing an opera. He felt *An American in Paris* was moving him closer to that goal. But in the meantime, he would turn his sights from Broadway stage to film—and that meant going to Hollywood, California.

8
IN HOLLYWOOD

George and Ira Gershwin signed a contract with Fox Film Corporation in the spring of 1930 for a movie musical. Movies had only recently added sound and were called "talkies." As far as writing for movies—instead of stage—Gershwin said, "I know very little about them."[1]

Before heading out to California, George and Ira worked on the score for *Girl Crazy*. The show included some Gershwin favorites such as "Embraceable You," "But Not for Me," and "Could You Use Me?"

Girl Crazy was well received when it opened in October. Gershwin said, "The show looks so good that I can leave in a few weeks for Hollywood, with the warm feeling that I have a hit under my belt."[2]

Ethel Merman, celebrated Broadway singer and actress,

said about the opening night of *Girl Crazy*: "It's very hard for me to stand back and take a cold, calm look at that first night of *Girl Crazy*. It's still thunder in the back of my head. I didn't know what was happening to me." When Merman began singing the showstopping number "Samson and Deliliah," she said, "Everybody screamed and yelled, and there was so much noise I thought something had fallen out of the loft onto the stage."[3]

George, Ira, and his wife, Leonore, traveled to California by train, with the Gershwin brothers looking forward to earning seventy thousand dollars for George and thirty thousand dollars for Ira. It was an enjoyable trip, riding in their own compartment on the train. There was even a nightly game of poker in the dining car, which Gershwin enjoyed.

While working on the movie, Gershwin, along with his brother and sister-in-law, moved into a house in Beverly Hills where famous movie star Greta Garbo once lived. Gershwin and his brother worked on the score in the house, visiting the lot of Fox Film every now and then.

The Gershwins had just about finished the score of the film, called *Delicious*, after six weeks of work. Gershwin used bits and pieces of music from earlier pieces. For example, the song "Blah, Blah, Blah" came from a Ziegfeld show that never made it to the stage.

Life in California seemed to agree with Gershwin. He hired a trainer to keep him physically fit, and he took

Ira Gershwin, George Gershwin, and British playwright Guy Bolton (left to right) work on the score for the 1931 film *Delicious*.

hikes each day up Franklin Canyon. He also enjoyed playing golf and tennis and going swimming. Gershwin got to hear the Los Angeles Philharmonic perform his *An American in Paris* in January 1931. Now that he had some free time, Gershwin worked on a serious piece of music he was calling *Manhattan Rhapsody*. Later, he would rename it *Second Rhapsody*. Before traveling back to New York in February, Gershwin recorded his songs for *Delicious* so the musicians for the film studio would be sure of the tempo on each piece.

Back in New York, Gershwin used some of the money he had earned in Hollywood to buy paintings. He also got seriously to work on the musical *Of Thee I Sing*.

The Gershwin brothers had worked on some of the songs while they were on the West Coast. So there was not much trouble getting the show ready for its opening as 1931 drew to a close.

Of Thee I Sing was a comedy—and a hit. The musical was set in the White House and opened on Broadway in 1931. Running for 441 performances, it was Gershwin's longest-running show at the time. It wound up winning the Pulitzer Prize for the best American play of 1932.

Gershwin now focused on completing *Second Rhapsody*, which he had begun in Hollywood. "Nearly everybody comes back from California with a western tan and a pocketful of motion picture money," Gershwin said. "I decided to come back with both those things and a serious composition."4

Second Rhapsody never became as popular as Gershwin's *Rhapsody in Blue*. It had a darker feel to it with a very modern sound. It premiered with the Boston Symphony on January 29, 1932. The piece received good reviews in Boston and, later, in New York.

Ira had recently won the Pulitzer Prize for writing the lyrics to *Of Thee I Sing*. But there was sadness, too, when George and Ira's father, Morris, died on May 15. Gershwin canceled a trip he was about to take to Europe and traveled instead to Havana, Cuba. There, he took a great interest in the instruments and music of that country. He came away from the trip with ideas for his next orchestral piece.

An all-Gershwin concert was going to be held in August 1932. Gershwin was composing *Rhumba*—later called *Cuban Overture*—for the occasion. He finished writing out the parts for the various instruments a week before the piece was performed. In many ways, the Cuban piece was the result of Gershwin's recent studies with Joseph Schillinger, a man who taught music theory in a mathematical, scientific way. Many popular music composers were studying with him.

Joseph Schillinger was a composer and teacher who used a system of formulas to show how a long work could be unified through melody rather than harmony. He had a bullyish personality, yet Gershwin took three lessons a week for one and one-half hours each over the course of four years.

Schillinger said about Gershwin: "When we met, Gershwin said, 'Here is my problem. I have written about seven hundred songs. I can't write anything new anymore. I am repeating myself. Can you help me?'"[5]

Music theory fascinated Gershwin. In fact, anything that had to do with music interested him. He enjoyed reading books on music history and attended as many concerts as he could.

His friends were always surprised that Gershwin seemed to know every detail about a particular composer or some aspect of music history. His record collection

Gershwin poses for a photograph in his home in New York City,
September 1934.

showed how varied his musical tastes were: everything from Stravinsky to Beethoven to Sibelius to Schubert.

George and Ira next worked on the score for a show called *Pardon My English*. The show only lasted forty-six performances after opening in late January. This failure was followed by a second flop, the musical *Let 'Em Eat Cake*.

Gershwin wrote: "Not many composers have ideas. Far more of them know how to use strange instruments which do not require ideas. Whoever has inspired ideas will write the great music of our period. We are plowing the ground for that genius who may be alive or may be born today or tomorrow."[6]

Gershwin had been thinking of writing an opera for a long while. When these two musicals flopped, it gave him a good excuse to take a break from writing show music for a time.

He decided to write his opera based on the novel *Porgy* by DuBose Heyward. Heyward was an American author, and with the help of his wife, Dorothy, he turned the novel into a nonmusical play. Gershwin used this play as the foundation for the opera *Porgy and Bess*.

In November 1933, word went out that Gershwin would be writing the music to *Porgy*. But although the announcement had been made, Gershwin had not yet started composing the music.

9
ON TO OPERA

Gershwin was a complicated man. On the outside, he appeared confident in his intelligence and talent, and full of energy and charm. Yet he was also often anxious. He worried about whether he would be thought of as a first-class composer. In other words, he acted the part of the celebrity, but he did not seem to ever truly believe it himself.

George and Ira's musical *Let 'Em Eat Cake* opened, and less than a week later, Gershwin signed a contract to write the opera *Porgy and Bess*. There was a disagreement, however, between Gershwin and the author of *Porgy*.

"I feel more and more that all dialog should be spoken," author Heyward said. "[T]his will give the opera speed and tempo."[1]

Gershwin had other ideas and told Heyward, "There may be too much talk . . ."[2]

DuBose Heyward

DuBose Heyward was born in 1885 and is best known for the novel he wrote in 1924, *Porgy*. Although he started out selling insurance and real estate, Heyward eventually left his business to spend all his time writing. His play *Porgy* opened on Broadway in 1927. It was very successful—even more than Gershwin's opera *Porgy and Bess* would be eight years later. Heyward also wrote the screenplay for playwright Eugene O'Neill's *The Emperor Jones*, as well as the children's book *The Country Bunny and the Little Gold Shoes*. He died in 1940 at the age of fifty-five.

There were other troubles. "At the outset we were faced by a difficult problem," Heyward said. "I was firm in my refusal to leave the South and live in New York. Gershwin was bound for the duration of his contract to the microphone at Radio City . . . The solution came quite naturally when we associated Ira Gershwin with us."[3]

Heyward continued, "Presently we evolved a system which, between my visits North, or George's dash to Charleston, I could send scenes and lyrics. Then the brothers Gershwin, after their extraordinary fashion, would get at the piano, pound, wrangle, swear, burst into weird snatches of song, and eventually emerge with a polished lyric."[4]

Gershwin spent some time with Heyward in Charleston, South Carolina, touring the southern city and visiting cafes and listening to spirituals.

Gershwin then continued to Florida where he rested before going on tour with an orchestra, hopping from one city to another. Gershwin also returned to Charleston after the tour was over and once again spent time with Heyward to discuss the opera.

Gershwin always seemed happiest when he was juggling several balls at once, and as soon as he returned to New York, he finished working on a piece called *I Got Rhythm Variations*. He had a week to get the composition ready before taking it on tour. Gershwin traveled with the Leo Reisman Orchestra under the baton of Charles Previn. The musicians made their way from Boston, Massachusetts, to Omaha, Nebraska, and then to Detroit, Michigan; Toronto, Canada; and finally, home again to New York City.

Once back home, Gershwin focused on composing the music for *Porgy and Bess*. The first song Gershwin wrote was a lullaby called "Summertime," which was also the opera's first song. Ira was helping with the lyrics, and he felt it was the wrong move to start off with a lullaby. But Gershwin refused to change his mind, and "Summertime"—one of Gershwin's most beautiful songs—stayed where it was.

The writing of the opera was spread out over a long period of time. Heyward wanted Gershwin to visit him again in Charleston since it was obviously easier to work on *Porgy and Bess* when the men were together. But Gershwin was committed to doing a weekly radio program called *Music by Gershwin*. On the show, he was able to present his own music and introduce listeners to the music of other—and often newer—composers such as Harold Arlen, who wrote "Over the Rainbow," "I Love a Parade," and "It's Only a Paper Moon." He also introduced songs of Oscar Levant, who wrote the music for *The Fabulous Invalid, Ripples,* and *Burlesque.*

While Gershwin was busy in New York, Heyward was working on screenplays in Hollywood. Much of the opera was written while the men were on opposite coasts of the country.

Gershwin often requested certain changes of the author—especially cuts in the dialogue. For example, Gershwin wrote to Heyward, "You must be sure that the opera is not too long as I am a great believer in not giving people too much of a good thing."[5]

Gershwin admitted to Heyward that he was not writing the music terribly quickly. Yet he said this fact did not worry him because he felt very optimistic about the opera.

In many cases, Heyward made his own suggestions to Gershwin, such as recommending that Ira write the lyrics to certain songs because it was important that composer and lyricist work together in the same room.

With this in mind, Heyward left the warmth of the South and traveled north to work with George and Ira in the spring. Gershwin felt that a light number was needed at one point in the first act. He sat down at the piano and quickly made up a piece off the top of his head to show Ira and Heyward the kind of song he was thinking of.

The piece had such a catchy rhythm that Heyward and Ira told Gershwin to leave it as it was and use it in the opera. The song "I Got Plenty o' Nuttin'" has been one of Gershwin's most popular pieces through the years. The lyrics were written by both Ira and Heyward.

Once Gershwin finished the first scene of the opera, he headed to Folly Island, near Charleston, where Heyward had a summer home. Gershwin took the *Porgy* manuscript and his painting supplies. Ira was going to stay in New York to work on another show.

Gershwin spent seven weeks at Folly Island. He had a four-room beach house that he was sharing with his cousin, artist Harry Botkin. The beach house had the bare necessities—very different from Gershwin's well-furnished home in New York. He used nails on the wall to hang his clothes, and he bathed in water that was brought in crocks from Charleston. His piano was a small upright.

Gershwin at times had trouble adapting to life on the beach. According to his cousin, "Droves of bugs and insects fly against the screens and the noisy crickets drove Gershwin to distraction, keeping him awake nights."[6]

When Gershwin wrote to his mother, he mentioned that the nearest telephone was ten miles away. He also said he spent much of his time scratching his mosquito bites.

When he was not being bothered by bugs, Gershwin went with Heyward to nearby James Island, where

African-American residents sang traditional songs. One tradition was "shouting," which was a combination of singing and beating a complicated rhythm with the hands and feet. Gershwin listened to shouting at a church meeting and, unable to resist, joined in, to the amusement of the church members. Gershwin listened carefully to the music that flowed around him, and he tried to duplicate much of what he heard in the opera.

Gershwin was very excited with how the opera was going. "I believe it will be something never done before," he said.[7]

Porgy and Bess opened in Boston in September 1935. The usually quiet Boston crowd applauded wildly when the curtain fell. One newspaper critic wrote the next day that "Gershwin must now be accepted as a serious composer."[8]

The following month, the opera opened in New York at the Alvin Theater. Again, the applause was huge. But the New York critics were a tougher crowd. Some complained that the mix of musical and opera did not work onstage—it was neither one nor the other.

Interestingly, one of the so-called "problems" with *Porgy and Bess* was that Gershwin had written such beautiful songs, including "Summertime," "I Got Plenty o' Nuttin'," and "Bess, You Is My Woman Now." Because of this, the songs themselves stood out on their own.

"I am not ashamed of writing songs," said Gershwin. "Without songs it could be neither theater

George Gershwin stands center stage during the curtain call of the New York production of *Porgy and Bess.*

nor entertaining, from my viewpoint. But songs are entirely within the operatic tradition. Many of the most successful operas of the past have had songs."[9]

Many critics did not seem to understand that Gershwin had tried to create a folk opera, fitting the music to the people and the mood. He had used many original themes, working them into the opera and then

Richard Rogers

Richard Rodgers was born in 1902 and lived to the age of seventy-seven. He was considered one of the greatest composers of musical theater, and was best known for writing shows with lyricist Oscar Hammerstein. Rodgers wrote more than forty Broadway musicals. Some of his more famous shows are *Carousel, South Pacific, The King and I, Cinderella, Flower Drum Song,* and *The Sound of Music.*

putting the entire piece in an American setting. It would be many years before *Porgy and Bess* was hailed as a great American opera.

After he saw *Porgy and Bess,* Broadway composer Richard Rodgers wrote a letter to Gershwin, and said, "Dear George, If you ever got a sincere letter in your life, this is it, and it's a pretty difficult one to write. There's no sense in my telling you how beautiful your score is; you know that. But I can tell you that I sat there transfixed for three hours . . . I never thought I'd sit in a theatre and feel my throat being stopped up time after time."[10]

Meanwhile, the opera ran for only 124 performances in New York, and then moved on to Philadelphia and Pittsburgh, Pennsylvania; Chicago, Illinois; and finally, Washington, D.C. Gershwin made no money off *Porgy and Bess,* and the investment of seventy thousand dollars was lost.

Gershwin needed a break after all those months of hard work and then his eventual

This is a self-portrait by George Gershwin painted in 1934.

disappointment. He traveled to Mexico, then put a few of his own paintings on exhibition at the Society of Independent Artists. In addition to painting, Gershwin played a concert of his work in New York. Then, it was off to Hollywood again.

10

A SUDDEN END

George and Ira left for Hollywood in the fall of 1936. While he was in California, Gershwin became friends with composer Arnold Schoenberg, who also was a professor with the music department at University of California Los Angeles. The men spent a lot of time together—talking about music as well as playing tennis.

The Hollywood musical was enormously successful with the American public. Movie studios generally had a full-time staff of musicians. After all, the musicals needed expert talent to compose the songs, arrange the music so it could be played by a full orchestra, conduct the rehearsals, and record the sound track.

The dance routines in these musicals were as important as—if not more than—the music. Onstage, at this time, musicals often had storylines where the plot was suddenly interrupted by a dance number. It was all part of the show—the costumes, dazzling sets, and exciting dance routines. But in the movies, the dance numbers needed to fit in more neatly with the story.

George and Ira were working on the score of a new musical starring the dance team of Fred Astaire and Ginger Rogers called *Shall We Dance.* "Something, even much, has been made of George's musical ambivalence," said Ira Gershwin. "That is, on the one hand he wrote popular songs and Broadway and Hollywood scores— and on the other, concert works like *Concerto in F* and *An American in Paris.* However, it was not a matter of leading a double musical life. He was just as demanding of his talent when writing an opening for a revue as when composing and orchestrating his opera *Porgy and Bess.* It was all one to him."[1]

When Gershwin mentioned one of the songs he had written for *Shall We Dance* called "They Can't Take That Away From Me," he said he thought it was "going places."[2]

The film was shot in 1937 and Gershwin watched as they made it—something he had never done before.

"It fascinates me to see the amazing things they do with sound recording," he said. "And lighting. And cutting. And so forth."[3]

Some of Gershwin's best songs are in *Shall We Dance*—"They Can't Take That Away From Me," "I've

George Gershwin rehearses with the Philharmonic Orchestra in February 1937, five months before his untimely death.

Got Beginner's Luck," "They All Laughed," "Let's Call the Whole Thing Off," and "Slap That Bass."

Gershwin was asked to write the score for another Astaire musical. In the meantime, he painted and performed in concerts. He also became a serious hiker and devoted much time to making sure he was physically fit.

It was at this time that Gershwin began complaining of dizzy spells from time to time. One spell occurred while he was conducting an orchestra in rehearsal. He seemed about to fall off the podium, and someone had to catch him. When Gershwin was actually performing his *Concerto in F,* he blacked out for a minute or two and hit a few wrong notes. He was examined later, but the doctors could not find anything wrong with him.

The next Astaire film Gershwin worked on, *A Damsel in Distress,* did not star Ginger Rogers, Astaire's usual partner. This time, Joan Fontaine would be appearing opposite Astaire. Fontaine did not sing—or dance—and the songs Gershwin wrote were written with only Astaire in mind. The songs included "A Foggy Day," "I Can't Be Bothered Now," and "Nice Work If You Can Get It."

No sooner was the score for *A Damsel in Distress* completed than George and Ira started working on the film *The Goldwyn Follies.* Gershwin had hoped to have some time for a vacation—but it was not to be. For one of the first times in his life, the energetic man complained of feeling tired. Also, the dizziness continued along with headaches, sometimes while reading and other times while he was playing tennis.

After completing most of the songs for *The Goldwyn Follies,* George complained so much about his head that Ira urged him to have a doctor give him a complete physical exam.

Gershwin was thoroughly examined in June by several doctors, but they found nothing. Time went on and the headaches became so painful—and Gershwin became so moody, which was not like him—that he was admitted to a hospital in Los Angeles to have a series of tests. Again, nothing was found and everyone seemed to agree that the headaches were caused by how hard Gershwin was working. They told Gershwin the problem was "all in his head." Little did they know how right they were.

In spite of how much pain Gershwin was in and frequent visits to doctors, George and Ira did not stop working on the score of *The Goldwyn Follies*. Gershwin tried to spend time at the studio, listening to the movie's conductor lead the orchestra. But many times he was too tired or simply felt too ill.

Gershwin finally fell into a coma in early July. Doctors had not realized he had a brain tumor. They tried to operate, but it was too late. Gershwin died on July 11, 1937. He was thirty-eight years old.

During Gershwin's funeral, the movie studios in California stopped work and had a moment of silence. Years later, composer Leonard Bernstein described Gershwin as "one of the true authentic geniuses American music has produced."[4]

A few years after Gershwin's death, publisher Bennett Cerf said, "Now, six years later, his music is played so incessantly, stories about him spring so readily to mind, it is still somehow unbelievable that he is gone. Because he graduated from Tin Pan Alley, it has taken all these years to convince some critics that George

Gershwin was a great composer—one of the greatest we have produced in America."[5]

The Library of Congress is the home of the George and Ira Gershwin Collection. Ira Gershwin devoted much of his time—after his brother's death—to organizing George's documents that have come to form the Gershwin Collection. These papers include letters, photographs, and original sheets of music.

Gershwin himself was a very complicated man. Music historians have written quite a lot about him—and yet the descriptions about him are wide and varied.

Some say Gershwin was a very private, quiet man. He was someone who was reserved to the point of shyness. According to his family members, he was sweet and protective, always looking out for them.

Conductor Mitch Miller, who knew Gershwin in the 1930s, said, "Gershwin was always sweet. He never raised his voice. He did not have a commanding personality. He was the consummate craftsman. Gershwin had a poker face. It was impossible to judge his reaction. He never looked exultant or distressed."[6]

Yet other writers have painted a different picture of Gershwin. They say he was cocky, outgoing, always wanting to be the life of the party. When Gershwin described himself, he would say he was thoughtful and often sad, the kind of person who liked—and needed—to be alone with his thoughts a lot of the time.

Will we ever know which picture of Gershwin is the accurate one?

The answer is that he was probably a combination of all the above. Gershwin had enormous energy. This is known from the comments of people who heard him play the piano at gatherings. Gershwin was able to improvise at the drop of a hat. He enjoyed the challenge

The Gershwin Theatre, named in honor of George and Ira Gershwin in 1983, is located on West Fifty-first Street in New York City. This photograph was taken in May 2007 when *Wicked*, the musical hit based on *The Wizard of Oz*, called the theatre home.

of making up pieces at the spur of the moment. He pushed himself all the time to be more and better than he was.

But Gershwin also spent a lot of his time alone with his thoughts, and they were not always on music. He had a lot of illnesses—or so he thought. He constantly complained of stomach trouble and dizziness. He claimed to have "composer's stomach" and often tried unusual diets to calm his digestive system. For example, he once went on a yeast and sour cream diet. When he would begin work on a long and complicated project, his stomach would usually get worse.

Although he was often at odds with his mother, Gershwin obviously enjoyed his family and liked spending time with them. He loved most of his life with his parents and siblings. Naturally, he was closest to his brother Ira.

But if there are still questions about who the real George Gershwin was, one thing is known for certain: his world was built around music. Without music, Gershwin could not exist. It consumed his thoughts throughout the day and night. Composing and performing music was not work to him—it was his life.

"Many musicians do not consider George Gershwin a serious composer," composer Arnold Schoenberg wrote after Gershwin's death. "But they should understand that, serious or not, he is a composer, that is, a man who lives in music and expresses everything, serious or not, sound or superficial, by means of music, because it is his native language."[7]

Music was indeed Gershwin's language, and he aimed to use it to reflect the American spirit. "True music . . . must repeat the thought and inspirations of the people and the time," Gershwin said. "My people are Americans. My time is today."[8]

CHRONOLOGY

1898   Born in New York City on September 26.

1913   Starts piano lessons with Charles Hambitzer.

1916   Goes to work on Tin Pan Alley. Has his first song published.

1917   Starts work as a rehearsal pianist.

1918   His first song with his brother Ira as lyricist, "The Real American Folk Song," is published.

1919   Writes his first Broadway musical, *La, La Lucille*.

1920   "Swanee," his first big hit, is published.

1924   His best-known serious composition, *Rhapsody in Blue*, premieres.

1928   *An American in Paris* has its premiere.

1930   Travels to Hollywood, California.

1935   His opera, *Porgy and Bess*, premieres.

1936   Travels again to Hollywood to write for films.

1937   Dies of a brain tumor on July 11.

1959   *Porgy and Bess* is made into a movie.

1983   The Broadway theater, the Uris, is renamed the Gershwin.

1998   Gershwin is awarded a special Pulitzer Prize for his music.

SELECTED WORKS OF GEORGE GERSHWIN

Classical Music

1915 *Tango* (George was fifteen years old.)

1919 *Lullaby*

1924 *Rhapsody in Blue*

1925 *Concerto in F*

1926 *Three Preludes*

1928 *An American in Paris*

1931 *Second Rhapsody*

1932 *Cuban Overture*

1973 *Two Waltzes in C* (published after his death)

Musical Theater

1919 *La, La Lucille*

1920 *Poppyland*
George White's Scandals of 1920

1921 *A Dangerous Maid*
The Broadway Whirl
George White's Scandals of 1921

1922 *George White's Scandals of 1922*
Our Nell
By and By

1923 *Innocent Ingenue Baby*
The Rainbow
George White's Scandals of 1923

1924   *Sweet Little Devil*
        George White's Scandals of 1924
        Primrose
        Lady, Be Good!

1925   *Tell Me More!*
        Tip-Toes
        Song of the Flame

1926   *Oh, Kay!*

1927   *Strike Up the Band*
        Funny Face

1928   *Rosalie*
        Treasure Girl

1929   *Show Girl*

1930   *Girl Crazy*

1931   *Of Thee I Sing*

1933   *Pardon My English*
        Let 'Em Eat Cake

1935   *Porgy and Bess* (opera)

Movies

1923   *The Sunshine Trail*

1931   *Delicious*

1937   *Shall We Dance*
        A Damsel in Distress

1938   *Goldwyn Follies*

1947   *The Shocking Miss Pilgrim* (filmed after
        Gershwin's death using unpublished songs)

1964 *Kiss Me, Stupid* (filmed after Gershwin's death using unpublished songs)

Individual Songs

1916 "When You Want 'Em, You Can't Get 'Em (When You've Got 'Em, You Don't Want 'Em)"

1917 "Beautiful Bird"

1918 "When the Armies Disband"
      "Good Little Tune"

1919 "Swanee"
      "The Love of a Wife"
      "O Land of Mine, America"

1920 "Yan-Kee"

1921 "Phoebe"
      "Something Peculiar"
      "Swanee Rose"
      "Mischa, Yascha, Toscha, Sascha"

1925 "Harlem River Chanty"

1926 "I'd Rather Charleston"

1928 "Beautiful Gypsy and Rosalie"

1929 "Feeling Sentimental"

1932 "You've Got What Gets Me"

1933 "Till Then"

1936 "King of Swing"

1937 "Hi-Ho!"

1938 "Just Another Rhumba" (published after his death)
      "Dawn of a New Day" (published after his death)

CHAPTER NOTES

Chapter 1. In the School Yard

1. Edward Jablonski, *Gershwin* (New York: Doubleday, 1987), p. 7.

2. Ibid., p. 8.

Chapter 2. Music Takes Root

1. David Ewen, *A Journey to Greatness: The Life and Music of George Gershwin* (New York: Henry Holt and Company, 1956), p. 41.

2. Edward Jablonski, *Gershwin* (New York: Doubleday, 1987), p. 3.

3. Ibid., p. 4.

4. Deena Rosenberg, *Fascinating Rhythm: The Collaboration of George and Ira Gershwin* (New York: Dutton, 1991), p. 3.

5. Ewen, p. 30.

6. Jablonski, p. 10.

7. Ewen, p. 49.

8. Jablonski, p. 11.

9. Ewen, pp. 61–62.

10. Ibid., p. 63.

Chapter 3. Tin Pan Alley

1. David Ewen, *A Journey to Greatness: The Life and Music of George Gershwin* (New York: Henry Holt and Company, 1956), p. 33.

2. Ibid., p. 35.

3. Ibid., p. 53.

4. Ibid., p. 54.

5. Robert Kimball and Alfred Simon, *The Gershwins* (New York: Bonanza Books, 1973), p. 116.

6. Deena Rosenberg, *Fascinating Rhythm: The Collaboration of George and Ira Gershwin* (New York: Dutton, 1991), p. 41.

7. Ewen, p. 57.

8. Edward Jablonski, *Gershwin* (New York: Doubleday, 1987), p. 21.

9. Ibid., p. 22.

10. Ewen, p. 75.

Chapter 4. Big Break

1. Joan Peyser, *The Memory of All That: The Life of George Gershwin* (New York: Simon and Schuster, 1993), p. 49.

2. David Ewen, *A Journey to Greatness: The Life and Music of George Gershwin* (New York: Henry Holt and Company, 1956), p. 75.

3. Deena Rosenberg, *Fascinating Rhythm: The Collaboration of George and Ira Gershwin* (New York: Dutton, 1991), p. 40.

4. Edward Jablonski, *Gershwin* (New York: Doubleday, 1987), p. 34.

5. Peyser, p. 87.

6. Ibid., p. 36.

7. Rosenberg, 1997 edition by University of Michigan Press, p. 48.

8. Peyser, p. 36.

Chapter 5. A Serious Musician

1. William G. Hyland, *George Gershwin* (Westport, Conn.: Praeger Publishers, 2003), p. 71.

2. Edward Jablonski, *Gershwin* (New York: Doubleday, 1987), p. 50.

3. Charles Schwartz, *Gershwin: His Life and Music* (Indianapolis: Bobbs-Merrill Co., 1973), pp. 55–56.

4. Jablonski, p. 65.

5. Isaac Goldberg, *George Gershwin: A Study in American Music* (New York: Frederick Ungar Publishing, 1958), p. 139.

6. Martin Bookspan, *TV Notes: Live from Lincoln Center*, September 1, 2002, <http://www.lincolncenter.org/pdfs/tv_notes/090102.pdf> (November 7, 2007).

7. Joan Peyser, *The Memory of All That: The Life of George Gershwin* (New York: Simon and Schuster, 1993), p. 81.

8. Jablonski, p. 72.

9. Deena Rosenberg, *Fascinating Rhythm: The Collaboration of George and Ira Gershwin* (New York: Dutton, 1991), p. 60.

Chapter 6. A Busy Young Man

1. Deena Rosenberg, *Fascinating Rhythm: The Collaboration of George and Ira Gershwin* (New York: Dutton, 1991), p. 124.

2. Edward Jablonski, *Gershwin* (New York: Doubleday, 1987), p. 75.

3. Rosenberg, p. 122.

4. Jablonski, p. 84.

5. Bill Adler, *Fred Astaire: A Wonderful Life* (New York: Carroll and Graf, 1987), p. 47.

6. Jablonski, p. 85.

7. Rosenberg, p. 119.

8. Jablonski, pp. 88–89.

9. Ibid., pp. 89–90.

10. Rosenberg, p. 119.

11. Joan Peyser, *The Memory of All That: The Life of George Gershwin* (New York: Simon and Schuster, 1993), p. 129.

12. Rosenberg, p. 122.

Chapter 7. Gershwin in Paris

1. Edward Jablonski, *Gershwin* (New York: Doubleday, 1987), p. 127.

2. Fred Astaire, *Steps in Time* (New York: Harper, 1959), p. 154.

3. William G. Hyland, *George Gershwin* (Westport, Conn.: Praeger Publishers, 2003), p. 116.

4. Joan Peyser, *The Memory of All That: The Life of George Gershwin* (New York: Simon and Schuster, 1993), p. 160.

5. Hyland, p. 126.

6. Jablonski, p. 177.

7. Hyland, p. 127.

8. Ibid.

Chapter 8. In Hollywood

1. Edward Jablonski and Lawrence D. Stewart, *The Gershwin Years* (Garden City, N.Y.: Doubleday, 1958), p. 145.

2. Ibid., p. 148.

3. Pete Martin, *Who Could Ask for Anything More* (Garden City, N.Y.: Doubleday, 1955), pp. 81–82.

4. Jablonski and Stewart, p. 167.

5. Joan Peyser, *The Memory of All That: The Life of George Gershwin* (New York: Simon and Schuster, 1993), p. 198.

6. Ibid., p. 73.

Chapter 9. On to Opera

1. Edward Jablonski and Lawrence D. Stewart, *The Gershwin Years* (Garden City, N.Y.: Doubleday, 1958), p. 191.

2. Ibid., p. 192.

3. Joan Peyser, *The Memory of All That: The Life of George Gershwin* (New York: Simon and Schuster, 1993), p. 231.

4. Ibid.

5. Jablonski and Stewart, p. 200.

6. Ibid., p. 205.

7. Ibid., p. 207.

8. Ibid., p. 215.

9. William G. Hyland, *George Gershwin* (Westport, Conn.: Praeger Publishers, 2003), p. 171.

10. Pete Martin, *Who Could Ask for Anything More* (Garden City, N.Y.: Doubleday, 1955), pp. 318–319.

Chapter 10. A Sudden End

1. George Gershwin, *The George and Ira Gershwin Songbook* (New York: Simon and Schuster, 1960), p. ix.

2. Edward Jablonski and Lawrence D. Stewart, *The Gershwin Years* (Garden City, N.Y.: Doubleday, 1958), p. 246.

3. Edward Jablonski, *Gershwin* (New York: Doubleday, 1987), p. 306.

4. Martin Gottfried, *Broadway Musicals* (New York: H. N. Abrams, 1979), p. 221.

5. John Haverstock, *A Volume of Good Reading,* "*In Memory of George Gershwin*" (New York: Simon and Schuster, 1957), p. 249.

6. William G. Hyland, *George Gershwin* (Westport, Conn.: Praeger Publishers, 2003), p. 151.

7. Joan Peyser, *The Memory of All That: The Life of George Gershwin* (New York: Simon and Schuster, 1993), p. 301.

8. New York City Department of Parks and Recreation, "He's Got Rhythm: Gershwin's 103rd Birthday Celebrated in Seward Park," *The Daily Plant,* Vol. XVI, No. 3460, October 1, 2001, <http://www.nycgovparks.org/sub_newsroom/daily_plants/daily_plant_main.php? id=10938> (November 7, 2007).

FURTHER READING

Feinstein, Stephen. *The 1920s: From Prohibition to Charles Lindbergh, Revised Edition.* Berkeley Heights, N.J.: Enslow Publishers, Inc., 2006.

Furia, Philip. *America's Songs: The Stories Behind the Songs of Broadway, Hollywood, and Tin Pan Alley.* New York: Routledge, 2006.

Reef, Catherine. *George Gershwin: American Composer.* Greensboro, N.C.: Morgan Reynolds Inc., 2000.

Vernon, Roland. *Gershwin.* Philadelphia, Pa.: Chelsea House Publishers, 2000.

Whiting, Jim. *The Life and Times of George Gershwin.* Hockessin, Del.: Mitchell Lane Publishers, 2005.

INTERNET ADDRESSES

The official Web site of George and Ira Gershwin.
http://www.gershwin.com

PBS series, American masters: George Gershwin.
http://www.pbs.org/wnet/americanmasters/database/
gershwin_g.html

History of musical film in the 1930s, featuring
Fred Astaire.
http://www.musicals101.com/1930film3.htm

INDEX